Intimate Nature

Z D Dicks

Intimate Nature
By Z D Dicks

Published by Black Eyes Publishing UK, 2019
Brockworth, Gloucestershire, England
www.blackeyespublishinguk.co.uk

ISBN: 978-1-913195-02-1

A CIP catalogue record for this title is available from the British Library.

Cover design: Jason Conway, cre8urbrand.
www.cre8urbrand.co.uk

Poems from this collection have been featured in,
As it Ought to Be
Words for the Wild
Ink, Sweat and Tears
Three drops From a Cauldron
Fresh Air Poetry

For Ted

I would like to acknowledge the following;

Josephine Lay for her help in finalising this manuscript
Anna Saunders for our poetic correspondence
The Gloucestershire Poetry Society and its members
And finally, 'Black Eyes' for publishing my work

Index

Intimate Nature

Alpha Male

The chimps bound and throw
thick chests thumped   waiting
teeth bared   rattling cages
behind glass   tourists hold fruit

The boss is cross   *Can we feed*
them now?
and *HE's in charge*

The keeper smirks
the old male   cross legged
de-fleas the troupe
babies given a check   picking

He ambles around males
grounded   away from flailing limbs
above   checks females   caresses
and pats them clean

The males jump from tyres
scream at the small one below
visitors chortle   *Weak*
he gives one hoot   the strong land
grunt   sink into clods
and cease to complain again

Ants

I used to think there were moles
in my grandparents' garden   one summer
grainy tufts of loose sods   sprang up like sand tents
scattered   on the bolding and shaded lawn

I asked   fending off a horsefly and midges
in the tangerine pink petrol dusk   *Is it moles?*
hopping size seven holes   to see the blind wrinkles
and claw shovels   on a break from their mining

Ted walked down half foot steps   just said   *No*
It's the Ants   and picked up spade and scuffed
under and through   leaving brown flat circles   bomb craters
smoothed over   scattering nests like seeds   to dry earth

The chink of steel   blindly   catching the odd loose stone
it made me sad to think of the colonies destroyed
beetroot and physalis colour insects   squashed
the genocides committed by that man

He cut through limbs   heads from bodies   all with deft stroke
but   if he were here now   I'd pass him my banjo

Bomb

There's a bomb in my head   with a hairline fuse
waiting   for a slight knock   to go off silently
no doctor or disposal squad   equipped
to dispose of this IED

Some die   their hearts clogged   caught   by an invisible
bullet   shooting pains blasting up arms
others torn asunder   by shrapnel   and fallout
not knowing   until the catastrophe
their wires had been cut   but my bomb is unearthed

The bomb that ticks in my brain   with every pulse
a war beat in my ears   that lulls me to sleep
inspires me to fight   blow people away
I'm volatile   and explosive   but not hidden in a bin
on a hairline trigger   this bomb is live   and so am I

Breakfast

In grey   an owl hoots   from a crackling tree
wings splay   and a mouse is plucked   no sound
but drops   from a ruptured rodent   that land like milk
onto crunchy leaves   on cereal   or the first touch of oil
in a hot pan splashing back to clouds

The owl hacks at its breakfast   stringy tendons   stretching
red bacon rind   freezing   it looks to the gold syrup
rising in the east   at the window   and the bristled man
in his white vest   who picks his teeth   scrubs flakes
from his eyes   a stomach pops like a travel tub of butter

Leaking over grainy fur   a pigeon breaks from chill trees
cracking through   like yolk from an egg   flapping
into shaded glow   to small orange bushels
a spattering of yellow   under black pudding sky
trickling to a scoop of beans   owl silently yawns

The old man taps his foamy brush   on a porcelain rim
leaves the single pane open   and a bird to sleep
watches marmalade sun spread   over hills and city
dabbing and dressing   he flies   to take a boy   to playgroup
and after   cook a fry up   with three pan chips

On knocking   his daughter's door   a tornado   catches
the man   a micro storm   at thigh height   *You're full of beans*
this morning!   small furrows   *No toast!*   climbing up
to a buckle-less seat   driver clunking in   he grins in mirror
this memory of breakfast   sustains me   as it did him

Carnivore

The room glowed a muted yellow   curtains
inflated in weft of breeze   ears pricked
and arms tied to bed   a woman purrs

Sneaking   out of eye line   a man on fours
feels for mattress corner   carpet crinkling tips
fingers pull up to knees and squeeze

The woman fixed on ceiling paint
pants as soft thighs cool   with night air
at the foot of bed   the hungry wolf laps

Saliva trails down split skin   savouring   sweet
meat   nuzzling   into wet gorge   he burrows
with delicate tongue   teeth spread wide

The woman convulses   a pool of wound
and tremor   her lover raises up to elbow
attacks her jugular   as he drips into her

One last death throw before black

Crash and Burn

Fox slunk   zig-zagging between metal
a racer slalom   through road railings
chasing pheromones   exhaust of pole position
the bars stroke fur   pressing him smooth

His engine pistoned in his belly
thrusting   towards a collision course
panting frost steam   steering to verge
to go up   in an orange pelt inferno

Over tarmac   pads rolled numb   run hot
a liquid trail   in his slipstream
melted and snow shod   legs prickled
with adrenaline   front end lifted

His rival in ditch   wheels spinning
up sods   Foxes horn bellowed   launching
onto number one   riding up a crumple zone
chassis' seared by high grade fuel

Each lick   basted hair and tail
in bush   roasted them in their pit
engulfed them   with barbs and flails
to their mutual destruction

Dissection

I am the surgeon over your shallow breath body
inspecting the sinew and peel of years   clustered in
muscle   clinical eyes connect worry lines   a hybridisation
of crow's feet and human furrow   under iodine perfume

Your breasts are pallid   as I pull back skin   slide gloved
hand around butterfly lung   careful not to touch
flickering heart   deft slide of fingers on organs   raw
gemstones still hot   in magma birthing chamber

I blind myself in concentration   mumble my actions
to reassure next steps   *find the entry wound   assess the*
damage   the bullet an asteroid   that smashed through
your mantle   slowed only by the centrifugal action of core

I open to watch the haze of mouth mask   sew with
fine stitch   rivers winding chill into pyroclastic flow
layers of blood   thicken to copper earth   hardened
by my last effort to seal a hole   an extinction event

You lie   gauze over a fault line   spun out of orbit
I wonder
will you drift and freeze   or gravitate   cinder
too close to sun

Documentary

On Africa's dusty scrub   flesh is consumed
lions bellow   and lock with barbs

In the Amazon   green sky drips   whispering kisses
resting on branches   frogs spoon on leaf

The earth is covered with merging cells
that divide at an alarming rate

A pandemic across urban areas
foxes scream at night   rummage in filth

Responding to flashing lights   the peacock
spider shows its dance   shows how to attract a mate

Octopi copulate with a special tentacle   male inserting
to head   and if bored rips off and regrows

Nighttime in the city   naked legs pace in a yard

I pull
howl   a dog on chain

Downpour

The class was over   three men remained
chewing words and rummaging
through syntax   I sat   youngest of the three
as they spoke of gratitude   flooding faces

I've made it to seventy   everything else   is a bonus
I digested these words   chopped sausage
and tomato sauce   ate them   his feather lite words
soaking heavy like lead rain   vision blurry

Like glasses broken   left arm tight and sluggish
as if sodden on one side   wet chill   with tingles of death
I write because I have to   not to get published
drenched by his first words   *everything else*

Is a bonus   the slow drip into a half filled tank
that patter wouldn't fill my years   my land
was cracked and broken   thirty five years   he's
drenched by a day   and I'm a puddle in sun

Enemy

I walk past houses   sun on face   loose petals
flood street   chittering children   skip
their lunch break   behind gridded mesh
on painted tar   a rainbow puddle mixes
creosote   dizzy fills nostrils   as I drift under oaks

A greasy-spoon scuffs open   sausage steam
clings to sky   unable to cloud   it settles
on passers-by   trees chatter overhead
leaves slice   pirouette   crackling on kerb
outside the florist   among stiff stems

Flattened   dust-mulch   a double decker storms
sheer hull cutting air   blocking reflections   a pigeon
judders overhead   rotor-wings chop   straight back
and jaw tilts   like a pilot   soaking up dawn
each step   locked on   shots fired   impact my back

A jacket off and   scorched   muscles melt
I fly to the park   wounded   to land on grass
lie   repair   and doze   ticking over   snoring idly
to rust and peel   defeated by a summer's day

Exile

A hooded shade of man   ambles up dunes
away from rounded walls   and locust city
sand   like dust snow fall   swirls   whipping ragged
umbra robes   whipping leather ankles and sandals

Under veil   a noseless statue   frozen   dehydrated
is painted   by blistering yellow   setting into cavity
tiny nuggets of ice   blow below deck   to rest
in the fissures of a hold   into a face disfigured

By public curved knife   unable to smell musk
he claws   like a lost explorer   mouth cracking *water*
with an acrid wheeze   flicking blood powder dust
breaking surface   a ship crashes into burnt beach

Rock froths as grains singe skin   lying in his arid ice
channel   the exile shrivels   castaway   resting into
curl   he folds for night   remembering air   lovers'
hand on neck   rose fragrance wash and salt fume

February

Snow thaws as it flutters   into fallen clouds
coating grimed city walls   wet brushing white
cobweb wisps   dancing under bridges   blackened
by winter exhaust   are washed by new current

Two cats   freeze and slow-whip tails
roads filled with waves of screeches
until windows are burnished bronze
and claws retract   their arguments split shadows

Crossings strobe their beeps in flat puddles
baying   cars lower fronts to charge
drivers shiver   plumb cheeked   and lean to wheel
micro tire turn   staccato judders to line

Drains chug and and gutters roar
as trees shake fresh sprouts   to flower
in broken day   fan out above   over thick coiled roots
in first warm breeze   at the quick end   of ghosted February

Four Seasons in One Head

Spring spun over chest and arms   petal bloom
pulsing from rough skin and bone bark
rich fabric   a barrier from cold   catching low
luminescence in weave of stems

Summer hangs   ruddy apples tied to head
grapes sat to side   like loose fuzz hair   wheat
draped as shaw   contorted around shoulder
knotted   with ripe cherries hooped through ear

Autumn spikes up   bold branches   a feral hat
forked   gnarled growths from crown   over
thin moss and remnant flutter   bled of chlorophyll
loose   in chill wind   dusted kindling like elderly pelt

Winter grows on face   thread   tuft and strand
protrude from cut nobbled trunk   chin bubbled
in stumps   eyes lost in brown whorls   folded
brow   wart bump wood   bleached by wind and sun

Four seasons strewn   weathered onto
one head   difference cultivated   until
half alive and germinated dead

Grizzly Sleep

A shadow at the top of steps
growls a lullaby   slinking pads
descend   sniff   a muddled
silhouette at fire side

Broken sleep with cracking eyes
chest heavy   I hibernate
fur spreads and teeth
mist   my wits half collate

A bear's yellow eyes
hide   behind downturned
mouths   a nose and maw
two fluff ears   all descend south

It rests its head on forepaws
and gorges on my dreams
eating away worries   that
my writing craves and needs

Its shape   blankets the fire
outline glowing orange   crack
quashing embers of my cave
radiating warmth
I dream an empty black

Haunted by Clichés

The clock struck midnight   and all over the house
clichés stirred   whistling   a train steamed and whistled
a chair creaked   and a poet rose
to fish and capture   snare and scratch out

An emotional rollercoaster   bounded down stairs
hit the buffers   derailed in the living room
bumped   into dead metaphors
sent the table flying

Ghosts of the past   drifted up from the cellar
eradicated by bright light   and dabs of white
followed by a raven smashing into glass
into the bedroom window   shuttered after eight

Floor boards undulated   as guilt
transformed   into a heart   the poet stamped it down
scrunched paper   and death knocked the front door
but the chess board was in the attic

Swings and roundabouts danced in the wind
under the pale moonlight   a howl   from a wolf
and a chill ran down a writers' spine
but the clichés kept coming   an irresistible force

Dawn broke   and a cock crowed
scraps were gathered   for inspection
critics would label the poem   *a good first draft*
not page ready   and the imagery *tired*
the words done to death   like a writer touched by madness

Hughes

My teacher
taught rhyme   alliteration
onomatopoeia   and to scoop a melon
he made me stutter a poem
a seventeen stone teen
he gave me Hughes

But   I favoured Donne and his flea
noting   that his tricks   would work for me
before   drifting to Poe   and his drinking
a guilty heart   in my twenties
chilling with Bergman   playing games with death

In my thirties   the raven flew
and a crow landed   cawing questions
as an outsider   a malcontent
made a nest in an aerie
and hasn't left yet

The house was shaken   a few years ago
by a giant that crashed   in our lounge
an iron man   we watch   read him
his wife   and their struggles
children cry   as they think their hero dies
my son asks
Does Ted Hughes still write?
and I palm a cheek

Icarus

A father gave instruction showed the joints
and mechanical struts over the flight path
cutting wind with fingers as if already flying
with a coquettish tilt his eyebrows wide
a tap on a shoulder pursed lip smile
he nods and points to a feathered rig
strapping himself into a shoulder harness
Icarus hoists and fumbles

The king looked up to the cliff feet sodden
sinking in beach robes dirtied by mud wash
two cheers sail over away from the land
and knife-rocks that cut the sky severing men
from divine rule the monarch hands like clubs
heard a father *not too high* *your wings will melt*
laughter battered the cracking froth
Never go too low *or* *you'll be netted by sea*

The king stamped a puddle as the men
climbed from his land and sovereignty
decreed writers transcribe
those who fly too high *dissipate in sun*
it's safer to labour and flap
over spitting fume *than crash in brilliance*
curses deflected down rock saliva over servants

Shadows impacted the horizon
Daedalus and his first born
flew for the first and last time

Impact

Hair flowed like golden silk
past lashes   stroking her neck
every look was locked   in my chest
sinking with each thump
there was gravity in those eyes   I moved around
caught in a trajectory   burning
to break through   make contact
glance over her peaks
crash into her warm magma
be obliterated   for traces of my fuselage
to melt   into her rolling heart
consumed   and she would feel my metal
smoulder   as we unified
at her core

Influence

I carry people in my head
all travelling from me
out from fingers   across pages
hitchhiking over white verges

Hughes sinks   drifting down like a balloon
into clouds   spying foxes and swallows below

Poe shakes me   well past midnight
demanding to be let out   to fly from birds

Donne wants to row through lakes
build a bridge to his island

Heaney just smiles   marching to his patch
sods flung   over shoulder   digging away

McLoughlin sneaks to the Loch
bobbing   palms slick with eels

The voices charge and dance
each pushing to get out   through a door
but when you are near   it booms and clicks
my voice bounds   and no writing is done

Ladybird

In bed   I felt a guest   a ladybird
cresting over sock toe   and I strain
push chin to rib   to the mountain base
black cotton   that is my heel

I imagine the climb   through
segmented eyes   and ganglions
feeding movement   the pull at elastic
the reveal of peak   and fabric ranges

The ladybird doesn't see a face
attached   to the country of head
as it sifts   taps ankle   clambers
over pores   like a hiker through trees

We share the sock   inside and out
both comforted   by stitching
but I bend   for a tickle in palm
knowing my calf   would crush shell

I unbolt the front door   prickled
with absence of warmth
mourn   heat not given
and sling it   to street cold

Magpie

I see a charm sat on grass
a magpie starts to dance   pick and feed
sinking through each impasse

On the path   dogs whine and pass
I spot silver   rummage   past a weed
I see a charm sat on grass

Late   I know I won't repass
and smile   at such a humble greed
sinking through each impasse

Pulling   I pierce my hand on glass
a ruby drops   I start to bleed
I see a charm sat on grass

Claret streams from a crevasse
I pull a sliver   but   it won't concede
sinking through each impasse

The magpies rip a carcass
and I drop the coin   and am freed
I see a charm sat on grass
sinking through each impasse

Notification

It's 9:33pm   and I wait
for a red light   in the corner   of a screen
I feel   like I haven't eaten   for a week
empty   legs rubbery and hollow
the blood booms   through my chest
air weighted   with misted hisses
my hands bitten   holding my mobile
I rest it   in my trouser pocket
like heroin or a magic ring
pacing   frosted black grass
tapping fingers on fabric
to check   it's still there
I need one hit   one message
and I'm hot for a night
to know   you close your eyes
backlight glowing   on your cheek
and you   are heated by a small degree
as   under red moonshine
you baste   in your hearth
and I sizzle   in ice fire

It's 10:00pm   and my phone is a block
No red corner
No ember   to keep me warm

Oyster Shucking

I slipped shell to palm   eased blade in slit   turned
and softly unclenched muscle   the petite
fold of flesh   plump with brine trickled
tickled down fingers   from small clean cup

Lids closed and head jerked   smooth on tongue
silk wetness swirled and engulfed
a delicate taste of copper rust and steak
dripping from mouth corner   lips flushed

The coolness of swallow   a warming of sea
on breath   sweet ichor gloss in cheeks
mixed   with saliva   freshened by swivel and
flick   a wave gushed   sinking swell to depths

I reached for another   masked by shell
eyes matching in silent dialect   rolling at mouth
you clasped my arm as I gorged   teeth bared
squirmed   as I took the last and stuck in my knife

Past Life

Before there was Africa   I layered ashes to my naked face
and danced a second moon   around tree high fire
memories of cloudless black   and ember crackle   sparks chased
grey   moving skull paint and limb flicker in shadow

In Japan   I was a light foot   low level warrior   running to guard pagoda
sword swipe filleting friend   inside   too late to bar door   pierced
through solar plexus   guarded child taken   lightless   unable
to shift consciousness to body   stamped by tip   cut by mid chapter

In China   my face swelled   hot in rags   pushing   with knitted thin arms
jailers   threw me in wooden bars   earth paced in torrent   like a chicken
in basket   poking beak out to mud   a rat girl watched me   starved
baying   stabbed through gap   I imprinted blood to clay

At the great stone toes of the Himalayas   was frosted light
I felt a flank of white horse   with laboured breath   closed
eyes and chanted   a monk's song of health   my hand circled on
its belly   I recited   robes alive with flutter   mantras lost in death

In Egypt   or thereabouts   I held a priestess   by a pool
inside   away from daggers   curved to slice tongue and
genitals   coal shaded   irises gleamed over my nose
with a stoop   sleek lips were tasted   no recall of execution

Eastern Europe   I saw my first tank   surrounded by a
carpet of rough fabric   gristled uniforms and drained men
as I sank   sprawled flat   listening to words   I didn't understand
slick with sludge gore on my front   air inhaled   tight with no
movement   metal creaking over and feet squashed from view

Back again   this time in barracks   different dress and tongue
subordinates saluted with full arm   my pistol barked at soldiers
and women   I walked the spring road   into farm fields
jacket undone   a few rounds left and my barrel screamed

This life I daydream   slaughtered by biology   scarred brain pressured
like an inflated tire   over my nose and pumping forehead
clenching thoughts   the smell of vanilla and cream   slow   bland

Poltergeist II

Two ghosts   grin   at opposite direction
one light like calcified egg shell   the other
translucent   black   smile fixed in thin skull
a deep sea angler   barbed   with blind eyes

Each neck is much the same   knot-wisps
that creep up to flower   muscles and sinew
a blade would pass through   their smoke-blood
dissipating to room   coalescing back to trunks

Both halo brushed   around bold heads   their
bodies   absent in shadow   merged as if
one   but the bleached bone phantom
has fuller features   cheeks fleshed by sun

Poltergeists   a duality   in where they stand
but   at their core   they are nothingness
an infernal chill   pulsed absent
cut   by a painter's margin

Prometheus

I gave my flame   to mould you
raise clay   harden your being
but   for sleight of hand   caught
picked at   slashed   by talon strokes
where   feather   caress used to kiss

The jealous chortled   that I
deserved chains   rattling the sentence
consumed by bird   but   the inferno
sparked   is white ember in me
sprayed from innards to blood grey ash

My wounds seal   shuttered away
clinks of beak   drip   quash my rocks
bring me to my lowest crackle
steaming coals   to breathless smoulder
but   wounds seal   and I carry the wetness

Inside   the forever sizzle   for sharing
my heat   running your supple clay
over fingers and just once   smoothing form
giving you life   cut every day for my betrayal
smiling in reddened torment

Result

It wasn't the way I held venomous snakes
their soft scales   how I felt hollow fangs
or   when Amazonian spiders   climbed over me
cardiac marks   spread on backs   and their rainbow warnings

It was in the embrace of a feathered mattress
the bites took hold   clamped into muscles
wrapping a victim in silence   as a beauty slept
and children stirred   open windows tickling like so much web

The neurotoxin sank   pulled me down with it
an invisible parasite   growing in my head
nestled in grey fibres   growing fat
gorging   on arteries   starving me of sleep

The brain scan showed a white ball
a ghost   who ate my memories   skull glowing
no bites or stings   from imported beasts   in a soft sweat sump
downstairs   I whisper *stroke*   clench through whiskey

Rose Cottage

A Tannoy crackles over beds
stirring bodies   from coshed sleep
nurses pin up smile masks
stretch eyes   their luggage hidden
thin veils swoosh and clink
shutting off a patient
tip toeing to a circle
whispers rumble
a doctor presses under jaw
purses lips and oscillates   his head
lowers to a watch   announces the time
a matron trots to a landline
calls down to Rose Cottage
and the sleeper is moved to the morgue

Scarab

I am king roll up the sun blazing life
for you raise and turn fire with legs
handle sand with a frozen grip and shape
earth to ball searching each wave and crevice

My touch warms the raw glass at your
feet kills shadow and slashes
a swathe through a blonde sea
radiates pheromones and revolves for you

You smell the solid soil scent come
to mound and push burrow face
down dig and are dug into morning
light swirls fluid convecting to sky

You will die there in heat my taste will linger
carry over dunes sink over everything pass
over until I reach lip and back again when
you will be reborn by my pyre and my kiss

Season's End

A gust   and a car alarm flashes outside
my mouth dry and bitter
rustling hum of traffic   sighs in the distance
fronds glow and sway with trees

Dancing ghosts shuffle   from a curb   shut a front door
wet breeze on my knuckles
streetlights dull   and clouds sink
they splash the road   into a puddles

A draught on my breasts
brushing my arm   curtains tickle wrists
inhaling low   my silk belt loosens
pulses   like fireworks   crackle on glass

My shape in the window   faceless
chills stroke thighs
seated on a wooden box   indenting cheeks
I watch trees bow   in time to my breath

Whetting lips   a tongue holds a thought   shuttering eyes
wisps float up   in this black sea
lines blur between lashes   opening
trunks jerk in the storm   like shadow puppets

Branches wave and lamp posts flicker
an orange white glow   or
a fire sparking   as houses are strobed
my gasps roll and trees grow talons

Hair blows across my face
soft   sleek   and scented
still damp   dripping behind my ear   down to jaw
words spill out of me   raining inside

I watch your shape   hear the gate gripped
twisting   leaves circle a silver birch
and a blade slices   around a bough

Self Portrait

The bedroom held fresh paint fumes
lifted from air   from open single pane
desk and bookcase planted   under
a grinning T-Rex   I tapped pencil to chin

Stooped and leaned to mirror
left eye scanned   pencilled to page
tongue   jutted to top lip   breath
on thumb smudging blemishes

I plucked the A4 and drummed down
naked   untreated stairs   embossed
paper held close   into pollen sun   emerald
sparkles   as I spotted my uncle

Teacher   Headmaster   he took paper
hummed   through closed teeth
I've seen better   It's alright
I slumped up garden steps   didn't see hidden smirk

I corrected   dropped   the sketch
to pigeon hole   for teacher to assess
days away   the sheet was placed
the whole years first score   in corner curl
9/10

Tattoos

It used to be   fine needles were hammer tapped
into epidermis   shaping totem animals   as if deer's
tendons   the power of their spring   was condensed
into ink   the bears muscle pulped and pressed

Men carried scars   as their history   illustrated
into first books   with stories bound to bones
each stab of spine   mixing black into blood
to linger   as a fountain pen   soaking at a full stop

The elders   deep lines in creased faces   held together
by the quality of their printing method   would pull
off garments   like dust jackets   crack hardback covers
and all would read   in reverence to a great tome

Now   these books are unbound   words ripped
from other libraries   the titles   on cover sleeves
not matching sealed indexes   scrawled and coloured over
defaced magazines   not remembered   no longer diaries

The Dream Wolf

I wake to black   raise hands to eye-line   turn
them over in imagined air   until lucid   hunkering
down   I lie on blue green blades   crawl as a cat
to mane of low hill and peek   ears pricked

Silent clatters imprint to brain   two samurai
armoured in flat orange shadow   strike   deflect
and step back in hover hop   in straight line   both
clasping   swords overhead   slashing down   I feel

Imagined breath   crick pretend neck   below   a white
mote   crests over an umber wave   amid grey fangs
and talons   a ghost floats in phantom wolf pack
fur   come to consume the haemoglobin of my thoughts

At the head   a cream blister   of plasma mist froth
bursts with eruption of teeth   I brush and scuff
dreamt earth in scramble and move as prey   galloping
in clumsy tangle   a newborn no practice of play

The swordsmen   stick to periphery
as I tumble over a dark   flat   plain   to escape
the silent howls   but am pinned   a feline stuck in maw
filleted by a bristled white wolf   and swallowed in chunks

My sentience   flows through ethereal veins   nutrients carried
in smoke blood   I settle into each course muscle   inside
hollow hairs   possess a beast   as warriors sheath and bow

The Feel of Velvet

I've never worn velvet before
the tufted weave pressed up   to arms
around midriff   or riding up legs   a silk mesh
that could   hold me tightly   like an embrace

I imagine it   as a garment   made to measure
scented and coloured like orchids   a delicate
flesh held against my chest   that would stave
off cold   if I fell asleep   outside   fully dressed

A perfume of fibres   that follows every stir and
turn   as I dream   a second skin   in every groove
of crevice and nook   tickling neck   like lover's
breath   warp and weft   the looming of two fabrics

I may never wear velvet   but   I can imagine
that downy skin   ethereal   and shifting   at a touch
a glossy ghost   that writhes with air   wrapped
close to shoulders   trapping my heat   easily

The Orchard

Down   past rough slivers of Cotswold stone wall
was the lower garden   reaching from earth
gnarled tendrils erupted   like arthritic hands   pear
and cooking apple trees   with sweet bitter fruit

The pommes were balls of mush   bigger than my grip
that would   I was told   rot my innards   at a bite   but the
pears   were rumped beauties   on thin knuckle branches
and I sunk into them   turning over with each swallow

I tossed each carcass   with its bullet pips   into log
pile   looking up   to the titan cherry tree   black limbs
beyond best jump   carrion cackled and bombed
leafless   in dark symbiosis   the birds a crow canopy

Evergreens rustled around   thick with brown and dusty
webs   owls and bats   roosting   side by side   stirring with
flexing flap and stretch of feather   at syrup blood
sprayed through air   and the clatter   of seed skulls

The crows were scalping those cherry nuts   cutting
blistered flesh with beak   I'd keep palms open
strafing to catch   a miss pulled stem   a spinning rivulet
of berries   but now   I would climb that tree   dig blunt
nails into bark   bend and rip   at the thought of hunger
roar   a shadow to sky   not wait for what falls to me

The Poet

I dissected the glossed book   walked a finger over letters
traced the contours of each metaphor
I was told to study the landscape
find the layers and tributaries   in those flat lines
experts had mapped the ground
mathematically measuring   each grain and angle
the slopes and residue   of a billion years
gridded and sectioned   in meter and rhyme
but my palms rebelled   dampened on dry rivers
as words flowed over the page
each image succinct   activating schemas
reminding me   of what was outside

I pressed the book   a monk at prayer
placed it next to notepad   let pen drop to floor
a new stanza was needed   to complete my work
nothing new would be written   in a closed book
spreading door with misty breath   I stared up
in the speckled black
a poem had already been completed

The Promise of Rain

Under static street sky
hard earth   swallows sound
a mouth   thirsty for a loaded
fork tongue   wet trickles from a
misted trunk   falling inside
leaf debris   musky fug of spring
heat doused   by swollen drops
earth waits   for his ripe lover

The sky reaching   shares
saliva   of coming summer
a verdant blade swells
with feather kisses   and earth
engorged   firmer   at her caress
is stripped   by glancing warmth
as   she pulls back   to hide in clouds
leaving only   an empty   sunny day

The Sunken City

Pink sun ripples on green roads as boats float by
shoals spill from skeletal legs and leopard sharks
hunt on church steps full songs rebound above
bubbled to foundations where God is lost in black

Lovers cradled in melon as one spoon penetrate
gondola purses and bags spilling over as coins
into fire-gore sinking gulps like fish food
to under-city with dusk flicker of summer warmth

Venice catches the wishes and the curses so deftly
spun in bubble froth the underworld of water
purgation peered at like an uncovered mirror at a
wake ghosts in gloom lapping in distorted faces

Each day the buildings creak closer to autumn
stains unclean growths sprayed over propped up
by hot air as swell gorges on brickwork burns
through stony roots to finally sink with crash sizzle
to baited oblivion and long dead kissed by darkness

Thoughts and Prayers

On the shadowed walk to work
spirits linger   a red glitter square
gets larger   by grey curb   the scuffed
foil   unpierced   holds its halo

Its owner   prayed for salvation
wandering the earth   in limbo
at the devil's hour   giving up
hopes   of holy union   flung

The packet   pressed and curled
spermicide   sealed inside   no head
for it to rest   stamped fresh
reflecting   aurilia   out of sight

I hold my hands and bow
pray   for those with venial sin
I walk   in widdershins   my ritual
complete   outside the orthodox
my   only   purgation   is the dawn

To Be As Talented As Burnside

She took Hughes   for a walk over fields
held him through forest   he showed
fox tails and badger stripes   husks of tractors
she left him in the porch   smiled him goodnight

Greeted Heaney in hall   after a day in the yard
patting face   she held him into the bathroom
where he whispered through bubbles
back smoothed   as a shovel under tap

She stepped out   towelled   dripping stanzas
closing on a line break   shutting door   *he*
stood waiting   facing away   she span him around
made him open up   softening his course edges

Oh   to be Burnside   and taken to bed
moulded to a chest   pointed corners
rounded   infused by glacé essence

Underworld

The walls were a marble façade that reflected
on veins pedestrians who lazily wandered
a clean complex at the back tucked in shadow
its veneer dropped into a bunker mouth

Neon light bored into sockets flashing
in skull it pulsed with crack judder of pneumatic
drill I staggered and fell into the maw arm
bracing handrail in grey staccato footed

Emergency bulbs at each landing dust settled
at rest on head luminescence stopped killed
by final step at the wasteland entrance car husks
were buried in a concrete cage and fire bin orange

The parking garage clattered with my footfall
flame hissed from manned drums teasing
out charred shapes twisting through mesh bodies
of long dead trolleys bandaged with rag mould

I stepped back felt up the strobed well past a tied up
spotted dog cleared toxin fume from lungs onto
civilised fronts where shoppers peaked through glass
finger smears lingering and I still carry smoke on skin
eyes adjusted

Victory and Defeat

My feet were light   as if in sandals
but   in heavy boots   on Park End Road
for the last time   a choke-chain tie   was unknotted
the report stated   I was   *An excellent English teacher*
a pass rate   of 96 percent
but Maths   *not so much*   decimated   *at 90*

An empty wallet in my pocket
no more KPI's   or   colour coded   spreadsheets
a vagabond   that blended with addicts
grey under an orange canopy
on a soft pulse   caterpillars dropped
and   crunchy   leaves sprinkled

They landed   on my ears
one over each   a half wreath of laurel
I was made an emperor   by a change of current
marching home   smiling   at being sacked

Viper Tongue

Coiled around a finger branch   bending
bark   muscle-rope thickens   to knot
fat drops drumming leaves   a crowd
of tears   dripping from chill of snake

Emerald diamonds fold   above
striped belly   horned brows   rise
sky-bound   to leaf clouds   as lead ball
eyes   pocked   with quick quash   glint

Its pupil cracks widen   as tongue
lashes air   density checked   between
globs   tasting   the wholeness of frog
ridges undulate   press into spring

An ocean of needles scratch   and latch
pump an army killing   two drops
dangling   like an unmanned hose
running off   down to mulch ground

Venom falls onto tongue   swallowed
like so much blood   mingled with soft
feet   and a stuffed amphibian   jaws
narrow   pulled back from grinning face

Spawn slick is held   on split tongue
after prey is pulsed   and pushed down
with each saccharine lick   a consuming
a murder of unborn young

Whisky

I can't sip   the way I used to   chopped
my mouth leaks   at a corner   sap from tree
warming lip crease   but   the berries
and smoke   linger on my breath   like campfire

Aqua vitae   carried to range glow   evaporating
up into after life   outside   to ether
but   when I try to draw it   back   my head
cracks   over left eyebrow   falling like a split log

I die a little inside   with flooding
tongue caresses   undressing hip shaped
glass   I drink the peat smells   earth
scorching burns   as it trickles throat clean

Distillers sent a single malt to space   it
came back tart   like boot polish   and just as that
shuttle   refused to let spirits lie   I let the flame
sink   smoulder and char

Writing

I close my face and my thoughts get fuggy
a drunk with dementia   I sharpen images
zooming   a microscope   into syntax
past blurry outline   sculpt my fluffy thoughts
with turn of dial   but   they are not grounded in a slide
they blow away   candy floss in a storm
before any grasp or compression in head   raw sugary nuggets
I scrape the sweetness   leftover from drum   make syrup mess
shape symbols and blend letters
marshmallow punctuation   placed in cavities
caramelised and swallowed
vacuous of nutrition
that will rot me in the end

By Z D Dicks

Poetry

Photo: Justin Smythe

Z D Dicks is the Founder/CEO of the Gloucestershire Poetry Society and Gloucester Poetry Festival.

He holds an MA in Creative and Critical Writing. His work is concerned with the everyday and of the very serious business of living.

www.ingramcontent.com/pod-product-compliance
Ingram Content Group UK Ltd.
Pitfield, Milton Keynes, MK11 3LW, UK
UKHW021037270726
13967UKWH00013B/2839